This book belongs to:

Made in the USA
Las Vegas, NV
11 April 2023

70468873R00083